IMAGES
of England

LIVERPOOL DOCKS

Members of the Mersey Docks & Harbour Board on their yacht, the *Galatea*, during their annual inspection of Liverpool Docks, *c.*1925. The chairman, Thomas Rome, is the white-bearded figure at centre front.

IMAGES
of England

LIVERPOOL DOCKS

Michael Stammers

TEMPUS

Managers and tug skippers of the Liverpool Screw Towing Co., probably on a ship launching day around 1950-1955.

First published 1999
Reprinted 2003

Tempus Publishing Limited
The Mill, Brimscombe Port,
Stroud, Gloucestershire, GL5 2QG

British Library Cataloguing in Publication Data.
A catalogue record for this book is available from the British Library.

ISBN 0 7524 1712 6

Typesetting and origination by Tempus Publishing Limited
Printed in Great Britain by Midway Colour Print, Wiltshire

Contents

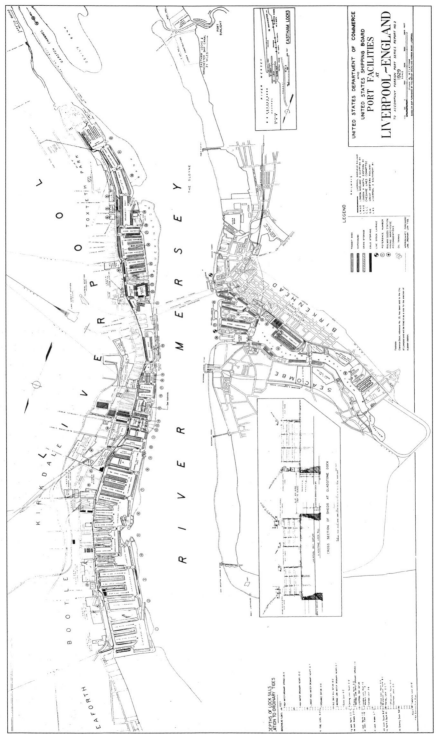

This map shows the two main Mersey dock systems, at Liverpool on the north bank and Birkenhead on the Wirral shore. The only major extension was the Royal Seaforth Dock opened in 1974.

Introduction

Before there were docks at Liverpool, ships were either beached on the shore or anchored out in the river. Their cargoes were ferried ashore in barges. This was fine so long as ships remained small but the Mersey has a fast tidal current and a high rise and fall in the tides. These hostile characteristics made it a dangerous anchorage and therefore, from the time when Liverpool became a port for large ocean going ships, there was a need for enclosed docks in which ships could lie safely afloat whatever the state of the tide. This time arrived at the beginning of the eighteenth century. Before about 1660 Liverpool was a small coastal port trading with Ireland. After the end of the English Civil War its merchants began to take an increasing share in the tobacco trade with North America and the sugar trade with the West Indian colonies. Such valuable cargoes were at risk without a safe dock and the first was built in the mouth of the Pool, a tidal creek to the south of the town, and opened in 1715. The deep-sea ships of the time were wooden, three-masted sailing ships of between 100 and 200 tons cargo capacity, but even this was a big increase on the size of the coastal ships, which averaged no more than twenty tons.

From 1720 Liverpool played a leading role in funding waterway links with its hinterland, first through making the rivers Irwell, Mersey and Weaver navigable and then by digging artificial canals, starting with the Sankey canal to the St Helens coal mines in 1757. Cheshire salt, Lancashire coal and textiles, Staffordshire pottery and Birmingham metal goods were all staples of Liverpool's export trade. This included sending 'trade goods' to barter for slaves in West Africa – between 1750 and the abolition of this infamous trade in 1807 Liverpool was the dominant slaving port.

Although there were setbacks from naval wars, collapsing dock walls and trade depressions, Liverpool's growth was such that by 1800 it was the second port of the kingdom and its five docks were a tourist attraction. In the early nineteenth century new trading connections were made with South America, India, the Far East and Australia and the long standing trade with the USA and Canada expanded at a tremendous rate with the import of bales of raw cotton, timber and corn and the export of textiles, machinery and emigrants. The new steam technology also began to play a major role. Steam railways improved inland traffic, steam machinery was used to build and dredge the docks and steam ships offered the possibility of bigger ships that could run to a timetable. Their increasing size had a major impact on the docks and many of the earlier docks were remodelled to cope with the increasing size of ships. In 1850 a 2,000 ton ship, whether steam or sail, was large; by 1900 there were cargo liners carrying 10,000 tons of cargo and passenger liners of 20,000 tons. This trend continued into the twentieth century, especially after the Second World War. Oil tankers were once considered big at 10,000 tons but by 1970 there were 150,000 ton tankers discharging at the Tranmere terminal.

The growth of trade and the steamship also meant that the dock authorities had to provide an increasing range of quayside facilities. Valuable cargoes had to be protected from theft and as a result high walls were built along the dock road. Cargoes were protected by transit sheds and bonded warehouses were built to house them long term. Hydraulic cranes speeded up cargo handling and refuelling facilities were provided for steamers. The port was also under increasing competition from Southampton (for passenger traffic) and the new port of Manchester (via the Ship Canal that opened in 1894) and this stimulated the construction of a special boat train station at the Pier Head and the improvement of much of the cargo docks. The latter were the backbone of Liverpool and provided regular services to all parts of the world. These included such famous names as Blue Funnel, Elder Dempster and T. & J. Harrison, which made Liverpool one of the biggest ship-owning centres in the world in 1900.

The port became heavily involved in both World Wars and many of its ships were sunk. In the Second World War the port was attacked from the air. Although it suffered a huge amount of damage it was never put out of action. It and Glasgow were the essential termini for the convoys of merchant ships bringing food and war supplies from North America to allow Britain to continue fighting. The return of peace saw a rapid resumption of trade at the docks with a substantial reconstruction programme including rebuilding two of the main entrance locks. The pace of change increased in the late 1950s and not to Liverpool's benefit: the passenger liners lost out to jet airliners – Cunard finished its Liverpool service in 1964 – and the rapid development of container ships meant the displacement of six traditional cargo liners for every container vessel. The port authority, which had been the Mersey Docks and Harbour Board since 1858, overreached itself by trying to fund the building of a huge new dock with container and bulk handling facilities and had to be reconstituted. Obsolete docks in the south system were closed and there was severe competition from other ports such as the new container port at Felixstowe to add to a whole range of local difficulties. Today, however, the port is in profit and much of the old dockscape has been transformed. Coal-carrying bulkers now deliver cargoes where there were once only handsome cargo liners, passenger traffic has revived in the shape of Irish Sea ferries and cruise liners, the container business, especially across the Atlantic, is busy and the derelict South Docks have been redeveloped for new uses including light industry, tourism, housing and shopping.

The pictures in this volume reflect the development of the docks, the ships that used them and their attendant shore-side facilities from the late eighteenth century to the present day. They are largely drawn from the archive collection of Merseyside Maritime Museum and I am grateful to the Trustees of National Museums and Galleries on Merseyside for allowing me to use them. The exceptions are numbers 26, 69, 144 and 145, which are from the Liverpool City Engineers Collection at Liverpool City Libraries, numbers 8 and 20 to 24, courtesy of the Mersey Docks & Harbour Co., and numbers 170 and 171 from Mr J. Parkinson.

One
River Approaches

The old approach to the Mersey was via the Hoyle Lake anchorage at the head of the Wirral peninsula. This deep-water anchorage silted up and by 1900 was only used by local fishing boats and yachts.

There were four lightships – *North West*, *Bar*, *Formby* and *Crosby* – marking the main channel to the docks. In 1922 the Formby lightship was sunk by the steamer *Greenbriar*. After being refloated she was repaired in Canning No.I graving dock.

There were gas-lit buoys as well as lightships and this picture shows one of these in the same graving dock as the last picture along with the Customs steamer *Vulcan*. The latter was used to board incoming ships for contraband.

The tidal range of the Mersey can vary by as much as thirty feet (10m) and in the sailing ship era dozens of vessels anchored in the river at low tide, waiting for high water and the opening of the dock gates. Note the two bathing machines on New Brighton beach.

The Leasowe lighthouse, which still stands today, was built around 1763 to mark the approaches to Hoyle Lake and the Rock Channel into the Mersey.

The use of suction dredgers from 1895 made it possible to deepen the main channel. The cost was huge and the Dock Board employed large dredgers including the *Coronation* of 1903.

Dredgers with a continuous chain of buckets were used in shallower areas such as dock entrances. The spoil was transferred into hopper barges that took it out into the Irish Sea for dumping.

Electronic communication made the river approaches a much safer waterway. Fog was a major hazard before radar. The port was the first to have a radar station installed and the present-day station monitors all the shipping traffic.

Wrecks were not uncommon and the Dock Board had to remove them. Their own dredger *Walter H. Glynn* capsized off the north docks river wall in 1910.

The Harrison liner *Architect* ran aground on the Pluckington Bank off the south docks in 1933. Unfortunately she broke her back and had to be abandoned.

Pilotage was compulsory for most ships entering the Mersey and pilot boats were stationed from Anglesey to the Mersey Bar. From 1883 they were controlled from the Pilotage Building at Canning Pier Head. The small steamer at the river wall is the river pilot vessel *Edward C. Wheeler* around 1910.

The Mersey was a difficult river to anchor in. Nevertheless, vessels had to anchor to wait for the dock gates to open and the three-masted barque *Gladova* is seen here anchored off Sandon entrance in 1907-8, probably after a voyage from Chile. Note the four funnels of the *Mauritania* or the *Lusitania* in the background.

The river was also used as anchorage for special events and naval visits such as that of the battleship HMS *Sans Pareil* in around 1890.

Most of the docks were built from land reclaimed from the tidal foreshore and were protected by the stout river wall. Occasionally dock walls collapsed as shown here at Manchester dock.

The Dock Board did most of its own maintenance and building works. This old Mersey flat, the *Wellington*, built in 1815, was used for pile-driving both in the river and in the docks.

The Mersey broadens out above the Pier Head and is three miles wide between Garston and Eastham. The upper estuary had a number of small ports such as Widnes and Runcorn for coastal traders like the Runcorn schooner *Snowflake*, seen here off the Albert Dock in 1926.

Another special river occasion, a visit by the Royal Yacht *Victoria and Albert*, possibly in 1897 at the time of Queen Victoria's Diamond Jubilee. The paddle steamer is one of the Dock Board's buoy and survey tenders.

Large ships need the help of tugs to enter and leave the docks .The Cunard cruise liner *Caronia*, coming in for her annual refit at Gladstone Graving Dock in around 1960, was attended by four tugs – two at the bow and two at the stern.

Two

Royal Seaforth Dock to Langton Dock

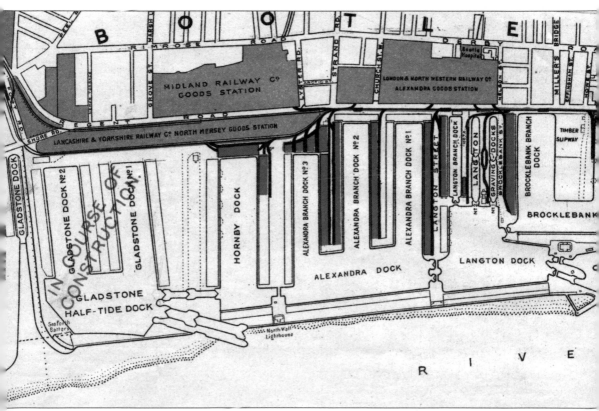

Royal Seaforth Dock, to the left of Gladstone Dock, was not completed until 1974. This map dates from about 1920 and shows the Gladstone Dock under construction with the isolated Gladstone Graving Dock, opened in 1913 to repair the large new passenger liners using the port. The Hornby to Langton Docks were part of a large extension which opened in stages between 1879 and 1884. Until the growth of containerization all the docks were used for cargo liners that carried mixed cargoes on regular routes to fixed timetables. Today some have been filled in or have different uses such as scrap metal loading or as a base for the Liverpool Bay oil and gas fields.

Royal Seaforth Dock has specialized berths for different cargoes, from timber in the foreground to containers to the left and grain handling on the right.

The container quay is the terminal for regular services across the Atlantic and to the Mediterranean. This picture from around 1980 shows the Harrison container ship *Advisor*, part of the service to the West Indies that has since moved to Felixstowe.

Containers come in two standard sizes – of twenty and forty feet in length– and are worked around the clock.

The Atlantic Container Line ships carry containers in the forward section and on deck with space for cars and large pieces of cargo at the stern.

The Grain Terminal can store up to 133,000 tons and ships can be unloaded at 1,000 tons per hour.

A steam shovel at work on the Gladstone lock around 1925.

An aerial view of the North Docks in around 1920 shows the Gladstone Dock excavations in the foreground and the Langton and Canada Dock entrances on the far right.

Almost complete. Gladstone lock was the biggest at Liverpool and at 1,070 feet in length can still cope with modern ships.

The opening of Gladstone Dock in 1927. The Dock Board's own yacht, the *Galatea*, was the first vessel to enter.

No.1 Gladstone Branch Dock accommodated White Star liners on the left and Blue Funnel on the right.

The White Star liner *Britannic* in Gladstone No.1 Branch. Note the large transit sheds with their roof-mounted cranes – the most modern design for cargo handling in the 1930s.

Gladstone Dock, 1956, showing how the quays were designed to handle both road and

rail traffic.

The North Wall lighthouse near Gladstone Dock. Its loud foghorn was nicknamed 'the Bootle bull.'

Modern cargo handling requires different techniques. This was all that remained of the transit sheds at Gladstone Dock in 1996.

On the south quay of the No.1 Branch all the sheds have gone to make way for a bulk coal-importing depot.

Canadian Pacific liners *Empress of Britain* and *Empress of France*, seen in Gladstone Dock, provided the last transatlantic passenger service from Liverpool which finished in 1971.

This Aznar cruise liner at Alexandra Dock in the early 1970s was bound for the Canaries. After a long gap cruise ships returned to this dock in the 1990s, only this time they were Russian.

Alexandra No.2 Branch Dock was one of Liverpool's grain terminals before the building of the huge new one at Royal Seaforth Dock. Shown here is a typical 1930s tramp steamer being discharged by suction elevators.

The Ellerman Papayanni liner *Mercian* of 1948 was one of their ships that used Alexandra No.1 Branch Dock on their Mediterranean services.

Hornby Dock used to specialise in timber but not any more: it has been filled in to provide more parking space for lorries.

Langton Graving Docks with the Allan liner *Parisian* of 1881. These docks have been filled in but the exotic pump house (on the left) still stands.

Unfortunately, the magnificent pumping engines used for emptying these docks have been scrapped. Only the 'barley sugar twist' handrails have survived.

Outward bound in the 1930s, a White Star liner with an Alexandra Towing Co. tug at Gladstone Dock entrance. To the left is a Canadian Pacific liner.

By the 1960s steam power had been replaced by diesel. Here, the Alexandra Towing Co.'s tug *Herculaneum* tows the Furness Withy cargo liner *Pacific Envoy* at the start of a new voyage.

Three

Canada Dock to Collingwood Dock

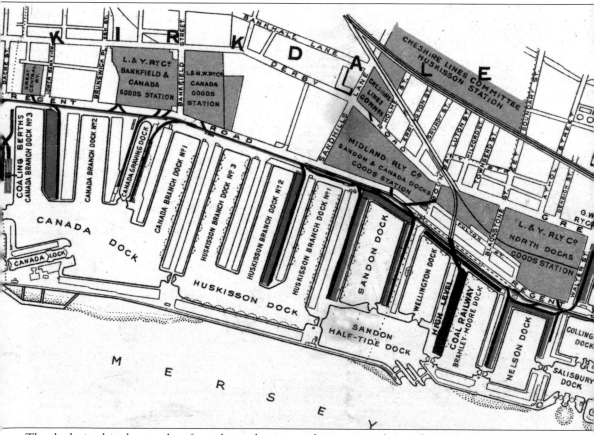

The docks in this chapter date from the mid-nineteenth century and were the work of Liverpool's most eminent dock engineer, Jesse Hartley (1780-1860), who was responsible for more than doubling the dock accommodation between 1824 and 1860. This group of docks has been rebuilt, a process that has included the merger of the Langton and Canada entrances into one large lock and the rebuilding of Canada and Huskisson Docks with three branch docks.

The seventeen-acre Canada Dock was opened in 1858 for the North American timber trade. Sailing ships were berthed bow-on to the quay to allow the long lengths of timber to be dragged ashore through their bow ports.

Canada and Huskisson Docks were rebuilt between 1896 and 1906 with branch docks and new, two-storey transit sheds to accommodate the increasing size of liners.

The increasing size of ships at the turn of the century meant that deeper water was needed in the docks. This was solved by using huge steam pumps to pump water from the Mersey. By the 1970s these pumps were obsolete and derelict. One has been preserved at the Maritime Museum.

The increasing size of steamers meant that refuelling had to be mechanised. Canada Dock had a coaling hoist that tipped whole wagons full of coal into a ship's bunkers.

Ships could also be refuelled by a floating elevator which is seen here between two floating grain elevators .

The High Level Coal Railway opened at Bramley Moore Dock in 1848 and coal was brought for shipment or bunkering in special wagons each carrying three containers of Lancashire coal.

The High Level Coal Railway has been demolished but one of its cranes was saved for the Merseyside Maritime Museum.

The rebuilding of Canada Dock included a graving dock 926ft long and 94ft wide, capable of accommodating the new 32,000 ton Cunard liner *Lusitania*.

Canada Graving Dock with the 24,451 ton White Star liner *Adriatic* under repair.

Canada No.2 Branch Dock accommodated the Harrison Line's cargo liners such as the *Author* of 1959 that provided regular services to the West Indies.

Huskisson No.1 Branch Dock was the Cunard Line's Liverpool base for many years. Seen here are the Brocklebank cargo liner *Magdapur* and the Cunard passenger liner *Sylvania* in 1962.

Huskisson No.1 Branch Dock, c.1935, a cargo liner dock at full capacity. A Donaldson liner

discharges grain into flats with a Cunard liner ahead and three White Star ships on the left.

The same dock about forty-five years later. The Panamanian tanker *Globe Constellation* is being pulled clear of her berth by two tugs while the *Parga* is discharging bulk sugar.

Before the days of containers every piece of cargo had to be manhandled on the quay and in the ship's holds. Note this crate is marked as bound for Auckland, New Zealand.

Jesse Hartley, the dock engineer, built sixteen new docks between 1848 and 1858, including all those between Collingwood and Canada Docks.

Collingwood and Salisbury Docks at high tide with their lock gates open. Note Jesse Hartley's striking octagonal clock tower. The ship on the right is a barquentine.

By the 1950s Salisbury Dock was a centre for coastal and barge traffic. The steam barge on the right is taking the dumb barge *Alma Bate* in tow with a Dutch motor coaster in the background.

Government grants to create jobs in the 1930s enabled the Dock Board to rebuild out-of-date facilities including the bridge across the entrance to Stanley Dock.

Stanley Dock, opened in 1848, had warehouses on each quay and locks to link the docks with the Leeds and Liverpool Canal. These dumb flats were waiting for a tug to move them.

Many of the canal boats passing to and from the docks were family boats and the women were expected to lend a hand and steer.

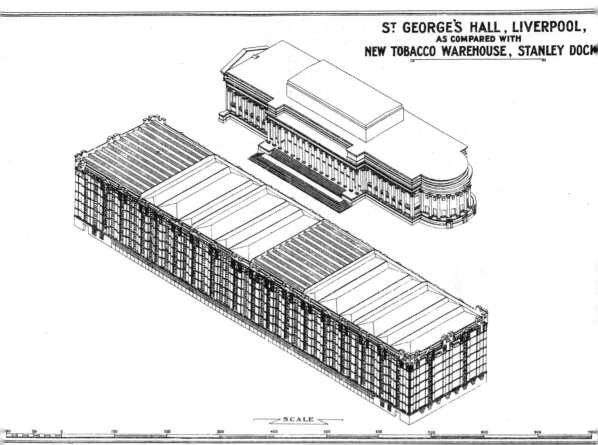

ST GEORGE'S HALL, LIVERPOOL,
AS COMPARED WITH
NEW TOBACCO WAREHOUSE, STANLEY DOCK

SCALE

In 1900 a new tobacco warehouse was opened at Stanley Dock which at the time was the biggest building in the world. This piece of Dock Board publicity from the time compared it with Liverpool's largest public building, St George's Hall.

Tobacco casks were brought by horse-drawn team wagons from the docks to the Stanley warehouses for long term storage 'in bond', i.e. without payment of import duty until they were needed by the tobacco factories.

Inside the warehouse the tobacco had to be sampled and weighed. The cooper in the centre is making up a cask for repacking the tobacco on the scales to the left.

Four
The Central Docks: Clarence Dock to the Pier Head

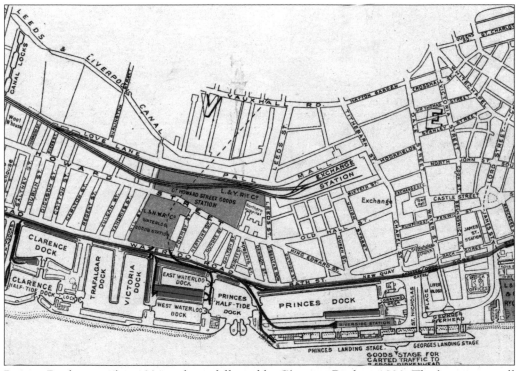

Princes Dock opened in 1821 and was followed by Clarence Dock in 1830. The latter was well to the north of Princes because it was intended only for steamers, which were considered to be a fire hazard to the wooden sailing ships in the other docks. The docks in between – Waterloo, Victoria and Trafalgar – were all opened between 1834 and 1836, such was the rate of expansion of the port. The Pier Head with its floating landing stage was the terminus for the Mersey and Irish Sea ferries and ocean-going passenger liners. The three distinctive office buildings at the Pier Head – the Liver, Cunard and Dock Office buildings – which form such an important landmark today were built at the start of the twentieth century on the site of the eighteenth-century Georges Dock.

An aerial view of Clarence and Trafalgar Docks after their rebuilding in 1933. The main Clarence Dock in the centre was closed to make space for a new power station while the remaining quays were modernised for the coastal liner trade.

The elegant, circular dockmaster's office at Clarence Dock was, alas, demolished as part of the 1933 reconstruction. The bell was rung to signal the opening and closing of the lock gates.

Trafalgar Dock had been designed for deep-sea sailing ships but by the 1900s was only used for coastal and canal traffic. A Weaver packet (steam barge) is loading sacks and barrels. Note the wooden transit sheds and the domed dockmaster's office with its bell and clock.

Trafalgar and Waterloo Docks were the base for Coast Lines. Their ships, such as the *Western Coast* (1919), had a distinctive black funnel with a white 'V'.

Coast Lines was formed in 1917 as an amalgamation of several smaller firms, some of which (Burns and Laird, for example) dated back to the start of steam navigation. They ran regular coastal services to all major ports in the British Isles.

Waterloo Dock, which opened in 1834, was rebuilt in 1867 with three huge grain warehouses. The one on the right survives and has been converted into flats.

The Waterloo Dock grain warehouses were among the first to use mechanised handling plant and here an experimental floating elevator is being used to lift grain out of the ship's hold and into the ground floor of the warehouse.

Princes Dock was the base for ships in the trade to the United States. Herman Melville gave a vivid description of its crowded bustle of the 1840s in his novel *Redburn*. It was still busy with sailing ships in the 1880s.

This print of 1797 shows the site of Princes Dock with the salvage of the cargo from a burning brig.

In the twentieth century Princes Dock was the terminal for passenger services to Belfast, Dublin and Cork. The *Ulster Prince* was the latest word in cross-channel ferries in 1937 with 'a luxurious lounge, comfortable smoke room and spacious dining saloon.'

The Isle of Man packet *Ben My Chree*, in 1927 outward bound off Princes Dock with the chimneys of Clarence Dock Power Station in the background.

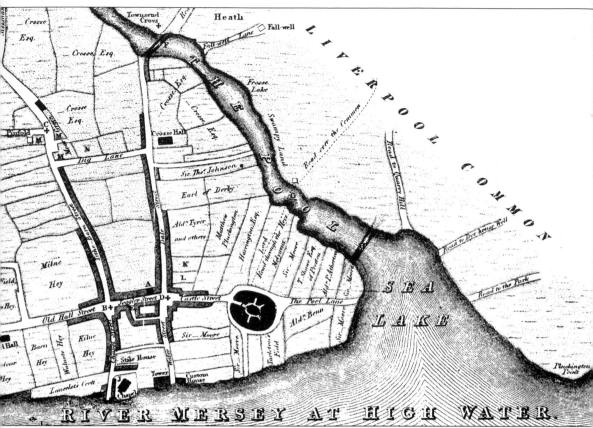

This Victorian map reconstructed the port and town of Liverpool in 1650 .The Pool was a tidal creek which went some distance inland and the present day Paradise Street marks its route. The Sea Lake at its entrance was reclaimed to build the first dock in 1715. To the left, the large, dark circle marks the castle and to the left of that, dark lines mark the buildings along the seven streets of this 'overgrown village'. The port area was at the bottom of Water Street where the Custom House stood (above the 'M' of Mersey).The foreshore in front of this was reclaimed to build Georges Dock and the Goree Warehouses in the 1770s.

The Pier Head in the 1770s with new warehouses and two new churches beyond. The two vessels in the foreground are Mersey flats, a local type of sailing barge developed in the eighteenth century.

St Nicholas Church marked the boundary of the old foreshore and Georges Dock and entrance basin were built there in 1771. The tower next to the church was a semaphore signal station that linked Liverpool and Holyhead before the development of the electric telegraph.

The south end of Georges Dock in around 1896, with two laid up sailing ships and the warehouse at Canning Dock behind. This dock was closed in 1899 to make space for the three big Pier Head office buildings.

Fresh oranges, lemons and grapes were landed at Georges Dock from small, fast schooners. Some of the cargo was sold directly to the public on the quayside.

The Floating Roadway of 1876 allowed road vehicles on to the landing stage to be carried by ferry to Birkenhead or Seacombe.

The vehicle ferries, such as the *Claughton* of 1876, were known as luggage boats. The bell on the stage, which was rung as a fog signal, has been preserved at the Merseyside Maritime Museum.

After an extensive dredging programme in the 1890s large liners such as White Star's *Britannic* could dock at the stage to take on their passengers instead of anchoring in the river.

Departure. Lamport & Holt's cruise liner *Van Dyck* is hauled clear of the landing stage by two steam tugs in the late 1920s.

A very special visitor to the Liverpool Landing Stage – the Royal Yacht *Britannia* in 1958.

The stage was always a hive of activity when a liner arrived or departed. Here, on 29 March 1919 the Cunard liner *Carmania* is taking Canadian soldiers home. They are being given a send-off by a military band on the landing stage.

Sailing time called for teamwork ashore and afloat. The mooring lines had to be let go and hauled on board.

There were sliding gangplanks at first-floor level to ease the passengers' access to the ship.

Hundreds of bags of mail were landed or sent on board by an electric conveyor belt.

The south end of the Stage was originally separate and this accommodated the steamers for the Isle of Man, excursions to North Wales in the summer and the Mersey ferries.

The Pier Head in 1914 was the transport hub of the city as it was both tram and ferry terminal. The liner at the stage is the *Lusitania* and there were two more liners at anchor waiting their turn.

The same view in the 1970s with buses rather than trams and an Isle of Man ferry instead of the *Lusitania*. The old landing stage had been replaced by a shorter one made of concrete.

The quayside, 1890s. Waiting for customers, perhaps, or waiting to catch the New Brighton ferry? The baskets appear to contain nuts.

An umbrella day at the Pier Head which saw thousands of office workers commuting to work by ferry from the salubrious suburbs of the Wirral.

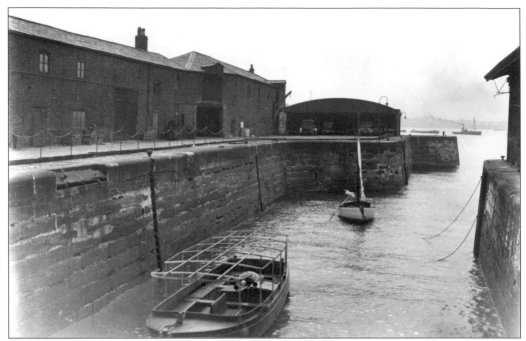

Chester basin, to the south of the landing stage, was an old sailing ferry terminal later used as a barge dock. By the 1920s it was the berth for a motor trip boat and a small yacht.

Manchester Dock was next to Chester basin and was a depot for the flats (barges) of the Shropshire Union Canal Co. and the Great Western Railway. Here, in 1929, it is being filled with some of the rock excavated for the new Mersey Road tunnel.

Five

Canning Dock to Brunswick Dock

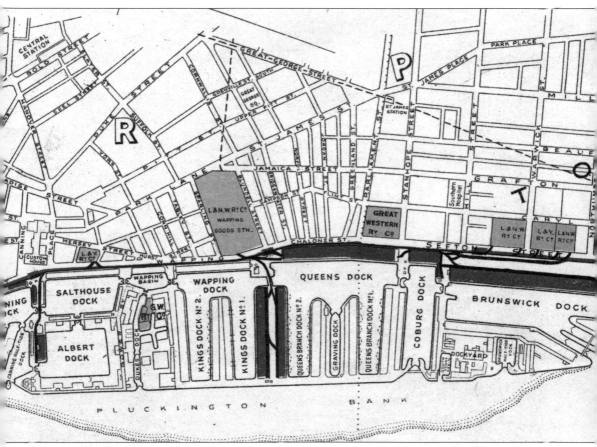

Canning Dock and its neighbour are the oldest surviving docks in the port. Canning was originally the tidal basin of the first dock and Salthouse (the second dock) was opened in 1753. Although they received some rebuilding in the 1840s to fit them for use with the new Albert Dock, they have retained something of their eighteenth-century origins. The rest of the docks in this section were all rebuilt at the end of the nineteenth century to provide extra accommodation for cargo liners. This reconstruction eliminated the last of the Liverpool shipbuilding yards. It also contained the Dock Board's main maintenance depot, the Coburg Dockyard, which could make or repair anything from divers' weighted boots to lock gates.

This slice of the Buck Brothers' panorama of the port dated 1728 shows the first dock crowded with ships. The entrance had a pair of lock gates which were opened about three hours before high water to let ships in or out. Ships had to be dragged (warped) in and out rather than sailing through the narrow entrance. The two ships in the foreground – a ship to the right and a brigantine to the left – are typical deep-sea vessels, probably of about 200 tons and 100 tons respectively.

Canning Dock was a tidal entrance basin for the first dock – always known as the Old Dock – until it was fitted with gates in 1829. This view looking north shows it in about 1900, full of flats and schooners with the Mersey Railway pumping station in the background.

Canning Half-Tide Dock was opened as the entrance dock for Canning, Salthouse and Albert Docks in 1844. A Weaver steam packet is doing a favour to two Mersey sailing flats by towing them out into the river.

The docks leading off the Canning Half-Tide Dock became the port's centre for berthing the last great iron- or steel-hulled sailing ships such as this unidentified, Norwegian, four-masted barque lying in ballast in about 1910.

The north quay of the Canning Half-Tide Dock became the centre for the stone trade. The schooner *Ellie Park* of 1879 is seen in 1926 discharging a cargo of granite.

After the Second World War the same quay became a depot for dredgers such the *Sifter* bringing in sand from the river for building.

In 1846 Prince Albert opened the new Albert Docks and its quayside warehouses. His arrival by steamer was greeted by cheering crowds.

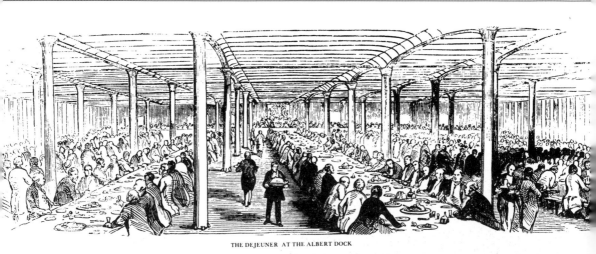

THE DEJEUNER AT THE ALBERT DOCK

After the opening ceremony Prince Albert and a thousand others sat down to a *dejeuner* in one of the spacious warehouses which were intended to store all kinds of valuable imports.

Albert Dock's warehouses were designed to receive cargoes directly from the ship's holds. By 1900 the dock was too small for deep-sea ships but a few cargoes were still received directly, such as this fruit cargo carried in a Dutch motor coaster in the 1920s.

All cargo landed had to be accounted for and the landing of the boxes of fruit (seen in the last picture) are being checked by a Customs officer to the right and the wharfinger's 'counter-off' to the right.

The warehouses had huge underground vaults for storing wines and spirits in bond until they were needed. The aroma of maturing rum, brandy and sherry was wonderful!

The upper floors, built up on cast iron columns and beams with shallow brick vaults, were designed to be fireproof.

Albert Dock was used in the 1920s for laying up ships such as the two steamers in the background as well as the Dock Board's salvage camels for lifting sunken ships. The camels would be submerged on each side of a sunken vessel and attached to it. The water would then be pumped out of them, bringing them and their burden to the surface.

The Liverpool & Glasgow Salvage Association's famous steamer, the *Ranger*, was berthed in Albert Dock between jobs. A wooden ex-naval gunboat of 1884, she was a salvage vessel for an incredible sixty-one years.

Hoylake sailing trawlers called at No.8 warehouse for ice after its conversion to a refrigerated store in 1899.

Steam trawlers were introduced in the 1890s and landed their catches in the south-east corner of Canning Dock until just before the Second World War.

Albert Dock served as a base for naval escort vessels in the Second World War but this is of a flotilla of minesweepers on a courtesy visit in 1937.

The huge loss of ships by enemy attack called for standard ship designs that be could be prefabricated quickly. The coaster *Barrule*, here seen berthed in Albert dock, was a Chant-class design – more angular than beautiful.

Salthouse Dock took its name from the salt works which occupied the site. At the end of the nineteenth century salt was brought down from the Cheshire salt works for loading into deep-sea sailing ships in Salthouse Dock. Note the splendid figurehead.

The north-west corner of Salthouse Dock was the berth of HMS *Eagle*, a former 74-gun wooden sailing warship of 1800 used by the Royal Naval Reserve until 1927.

In its heyday Salthouse Dock was used for loading sailing ships which had discharged their imports into the Albert Dock warehouses and had to be loaded with exports. The more distant ports of the world such as those of Australia and New Zealand were served by regular sailing ship services until the 1880s.

Although sailing ships looked beautiful, life on board was invariably hard. The *Leicester Castle*, seen here lying in Salthouse Dock, suffered a mutiny in 1902 in which the captain was wounded and the second mate killed.

Wapping Dock was opened in 1855. Like the Albert Dock its warehouse was equipped with hydraulic cranes (in the elliptical arched openings) to speed up cargo handling.

King's Dock's two-storey transit shed of 1906 was fitted with roof-mounted cranes to help shift cargoes. Note the absence of a guard rail on the walkway.

Queen's Dock, opened in 1796 and rebuilt between 1901 and 1906, was one of the docks that handled imported timber, possibly because of the yards on its foreshore where wooden ships were built.

The sailing ship *Jhelum*, built by Joseph Steel & Son in 1849 at Queen's Dock, survives to this day as a hulk at Stanley in the Falkland Islands.

Yeoward Brothers were shipowners with a regular service to the Canaries. They brought in large quantities of fresh fruit, oranges in this case, to either King's or Coburg docks.

Once the cases of oranges were landed they were temporarily stored in the quayside transit shed. Samples were taken and auction sales conducted at the Liverpool Fruit Exchange.

Coburg Dockyard employed hundreds of skilled workers, some of whom are seen queuing to receive their pay in 1902. Ordinary dock labourers were casually employed and were taken on for half a day at a time according to demand.

Brunswick Dock, 16 August 1923, with three Harrison liners loading cargo for India, East Africa or the West Indies from the transit sheds and from barges.

Grain became one of the biggest imports after 1850 because of the increasing urban population. A new granary was built at Coburg in 1906 and this second was added next to it in 1932. Here, grain is being discharged from barges that have carried it from the deep-water docks to the north. The *Elmarine* (right) was built from reinforced concrete.

Brunswick Dock was opened in 1832 for the timber trade. It was rebuilt between 1900 and 1908 as a cargo liner dock with big locks. Its old, small graving docks were demolished and a new reinforced-concrete wall can be seen under construction.

More rebuilding was required after the bombing of the docks in the Second World War. This picture shows the extensive damage at Brunswick Dock and Coburg Dockyard in 1941.

Six

Toxteth Dock to Garston Dock

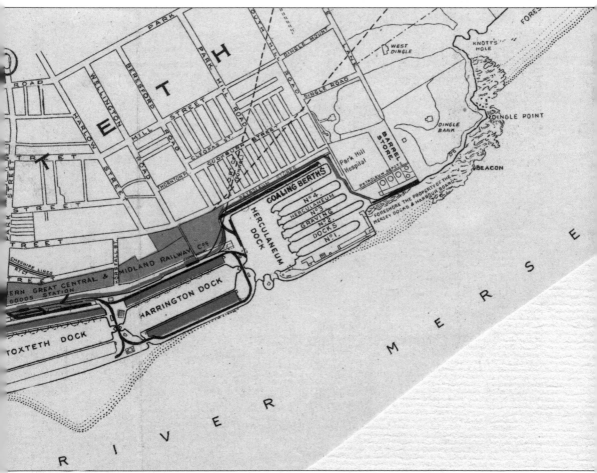

Liverpool's monopoly of the lower Mersey traffic was threatened by rival developments at Harrington Dock (to the south of Brunswick Dock) in 1839, Birkenhead in 1844 and Garston in 1853. Both the Harrington and the Birkenhead developments were taken over by the Liverpool authorities, while Garston, which was promoted by the London North Western Railway, has remained independent. Unfortunately, Garston is sited too far away from Liverpool's south docks to be included in this map.

Toxteth dock was opened in 1888 and took its name from the adjacent suburb. The origins of the name go back to Viking times when it was Toca's staithe (landing place). It was used by both by Harrison and Elder Dempster lines. Harrington Dock, opened in 1883, was a similar cargo liner dock and its entrance was in the centre of the picture.

Elder Dempster Lines specialised in the West African trade and as a result imported large quantities of palm oil for making soap and margarine. Until the 1930s it was carried in large wooden barrels. This somewhat antique form of cargo carrying was handled with the latest electric travelling crane and Sentinel steam lorry when it arrived at Harrington Dock.

Horse-drawn transport was still economical into the 1950s for short hauls between the docks, warehouses and railway goods depots. Pickering's motor lorry is outnumbered by the team wagons in this busy 1920s scene at Harrington Dock.

Every bale, bundle, barrel or box had to be manhandled from wagon to transit shed, then slung for hoisting into the ship's hold where it had again to be manhandled into position. Elder Dempsters shipped thousands of bales of Lancashire cotton like this one to West Africa.

Herculaneum Dock was completed in 1866 and had four graving docks, a coal depot and, later, oil storage facilities.

Herculaneun Dock took its name from its predecessor, the famous Liverpool Herculaneum pottery which was noted for its transfer creamwares. Much of its production was exported and many of its pieces had nautical motifs such as this jug with the sailor's wife waving him farewell as his ship sails.

Herculaneum Dock had been the first oil storage depot at Liverpool. By the 1920s this traffic had outgrown its capacity and a new river jetty for tankers was opened just to the south in 1923.

By the end of the Second World War the Dingle oil terminal had become too small for the increasing size of tankers and in 1960 a large new deep-water terminal was opened at Tranmere on the opposite bank of the river. It remains in use today.

Garston Docks were opened in 1853, chiefly for the shipment of coal brought down from the inland coal mines of Lancashire. This view of around 1890 shows a Scandinavian-built barque on the left and four Mersey sailing flats alongside the coal tips.

The coal-filled railway trucks were shunted on to the coal hoists at high level and upended to shoot the coal straight into the ship's holds (making a huge cloud of dust!) The steamer *Beatrice*, built in 1889 and owned in Dublin, was probably taking coal for the Irish capital.

The Mersey estuary above Garston becomes increasingly shallow and is only accessible to shallow draft vessels like Mersey sailing flats. This pair are, in fact, loading sand from an offshore sandbank somewhere inland of Garston around 1910.

The Garston shore was also used for shipbreaking and in 1978 the last two steamers on the Mersey, the Dock Board's buoy and salvage tenders *Vigilant* (renamed *Staunch* in her final months) and *Salvor*, were broken up here.

Seven
Along the Dock Road

The docks were surrounded by high walls to protect the valuable cargoes from theft, giving them the appearance of fortifications. The harsh character of this streetscape was reinforced by the granite setts that paved the 'dock road'.

Dock walls were expensive to build and many docks remained open. This is Georges Dock basin in around 1860 with a heavy wagon from the Windsor Iron Foundry, one of the many maritime engineering firms around the port.

Jesse Hartley used some of the motifs of medieval castles in his dock wall building, including this fantastic policeman's hut at the entrance to Wapping Dock .

Canning-Georges Dock passage, known as 'Nova Scotia', had a mixture of occupants, including a salt store, pubs and a ship's block maker, that reflected the eighteenth-century rather than the late nineteenth-century port.

Much of the paperwork linked to ships and cargoes flowed to and from the magnificent Customs House built on the site of the Old Dock and demolished after bomb damage at the end of the Second World War.

The Albert Dock Traffic Office was another temple of commerce, but with a cast iron pediment and columns to reflect its modernity in 1846.

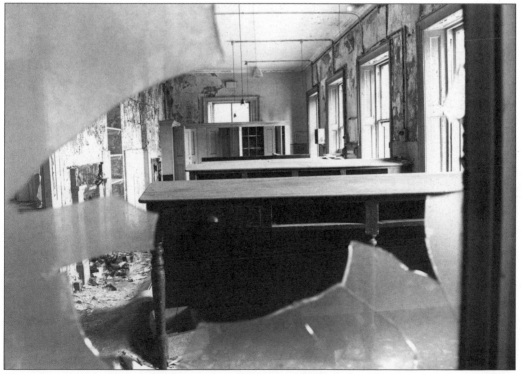

However, its interior was Dickensian, with rows of high desks. The busy clerks had long departed when this derelict relic was recorded in 1974.

A panoramic view of the dock road to the south of the Pier Head in around 1914 with the new Dock Board office to the right, the overhead railway in the centre and the old Goree Warehouses to the left.

The great trio of waterfront offices – from left to right, the Liver Building (1911), the Cunard Building (1916) and the Dock Office (1907) – stood for the prestige of the port in the early twentieth century and are still Liverpool icons today.

The one fixed point in the landscape of the dock road has been St Nicholas' parish church of Liverpool. Originally built around 1360 it has undergone various rebuildings, but always on the same site. Unfortunately, its beautiful tower is today overshadowed by tall, modern buildings.

Much of the shipping business of the port was conducted at Exchange Flags, uphill from the Pier Head. This was a gathering place for shipowners, brokers, merchants and anyone who had business for the docks.

Liverpool was also the centre of a major marine insurance business because of the large numbers of locally owned ships and the huge volumes of cargo shipped. The State Assurance Co. has long been taken over and its offices are now a nightclub.

In around 1860 the dock road opposite Georges Dock was congested with carts and wagons just as the dock was full of sailing ships.

In the heyday of the sailing ships Liverpool had a visiting population of up to 10,000 sailors. Many were exploited by the local people and the Sailor's Home was therefore established in 1851 to provide them with cheap, wholesome accommodation.

Liverpool had a reputation as a good place for sailors to enjoy themselves and there were pubs all along the dock road. This unnamed pub of the 1920s has a tiled, austere style except for the magnificent oil painting of a steamer in stormy weather.

There were so many ships in Liverpool Docks that painting their portraits provided a living for a whole range of local artists. The best, such as Samuel Walters, had their work shown at the Royal Academy but others produced accurate portraits, such as this one of the four-masted ship *Liverpool*, to a less academic style and much more cheaply.

The dock road was being continually extended to keep up with the building of new docks. It had various names according to its locality. These timber yards are on Regent Road, over the Liverpool boundary in the borough of Bootle.

Much of the inland side of Regent Road was covered in timber yards. The workers in this view are manning a hand-powered travelling crane to lift large baulks of tropical hardwood from the wagon.

Processing industries using imported raw materials were also sited along the dock road. These included the Tate and Lyle sugar refinery. In 1957 they built a huge new raw cane sugar store, which was linked to Huskisson Dock by a conveyor belt across the road.

The Directors of Tate and Lyle were photographed in its cavernous interior during its official opening in 1957.

Wooden barrels were once essential packaging for liquids and solids and many were made or repaired in cooperages close to the docks. Their use persisted for a long time and James Greig, for example, was still making them in the 1960s when he had this advertisement printed.

Docks traffic in 1919 in the Goree and James Street. Note the two-horse team wagons, the steam wagon in the foreground and the headquarters of the White Star Line to the right.

Opposite: Rum and other spirits were imported in large quantities and much of it was bottled in the local bonded warehouses. This view is at Albert Dock.

The port also received and despatched goods inland via the Leeds and Liverpool Canal. By the 1960s its traffic was mainly restricted to coal boats for the gasworks and Tate and Lyle's sugar refinery.

The entrance of the canal company's offices in Pall Mall carried the badges of both cities and was a victim of the wartime bombs.

The dock railway handled goods traffic while between 1893 and 1956 the Liverpool Overhead Railway above carried passengers. In 1957 the overhead track was being demolished while the small saddle tank engines below still delivered trucks to the docks.

Steam lorries were still very much in evidence on the docks until the early 1960s and the United Africa Company had a large fleet of Sentinel types like this one, built about 1925.

Diesel lorries parked over the railway tracks at what is now the Maritime Museum Building at Albert Dock symbolise the dominance of road transport over rail by the 1960s.

Unitised loads that could be carried by ship, road or rail first made an impact in the late 1950s. This Coast Lines advertisement of 1957 is an early example of what is now the predominant method of transporting mixed cargoes, i.e. in standard-size boxes and tanks.

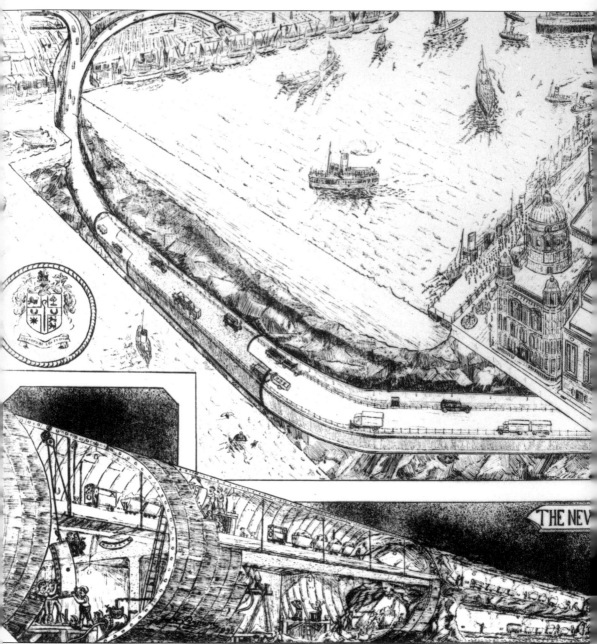

The opening of the first Mersey road tunnel in 1934 provided a much more efficient link

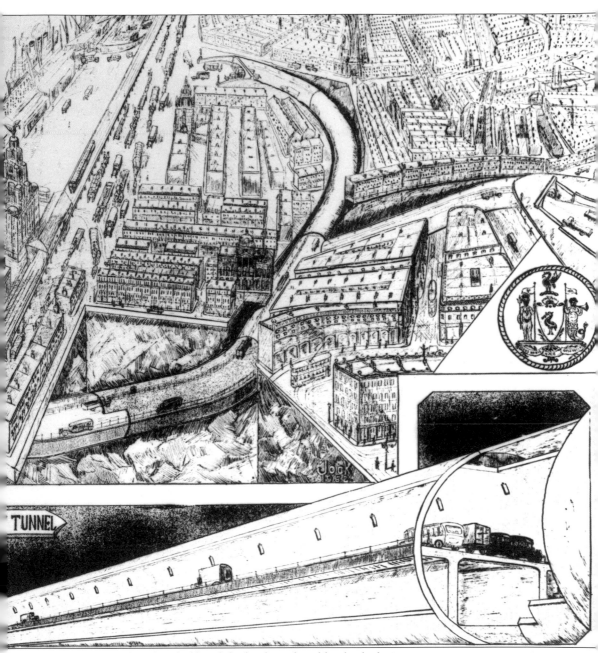

TUNNEL

between Liverpool and Birkenhead docks than the old vehicle ferries.

Today the 'dock road' has lost much of its Victorian character. Most of the dockside pubs, for example, have been closed or, in the case of the attractive A1 at Lloyds, demolished.

This office building of 1863 has become a lorry driver's cafe with a satellite dish on the parapet.

Eight

Old Docks, New Uses

In 1981 the Albert Dock Traffic Office was no more than a derelict shell. This was the year in which the Merseyside Development Corporation was established by the Government to take over the South Docks area, rebuild the infrastructure and find new users. The Traffic Office became the hi-tech news studio for Granada, the local TV company.

The state of Albert Dock in 1981 was deplorable: the dock was full of mud, some of the quay walls were collapsing and all the Grade One listed warehouses were derelict.

By the summer of 1984 all the mud had been dredged away. The first ship to re-enter was the Weaver packet *Wincham*. Note the construction work on the Maritime Museum and the Traffic Office in the background.

The same dereliction applied at Canning Dock, where the old 1820s swing bridge at the end of the dock was smothered in weeds. The modern office to the left was built on the site of the first dock.

This similar view dates from 1997, during the weekend of the Mersey River Festival.

Once, every dock entrance had a residence for the Piermaster who controlled the dock. This one, at Albert Dock, was on the point of collapse in 1981.

By 1984 it had been rebuilt and refurnished as it used to be. Mrs Cleator (extreme left), Mrs Parry (third left) and Mr Jameson (extreme right) all lived in the house as children and contributed invaluable memories of its interiors.

The South Docks were the oldest, least modernised in the whole Liverpool system and as a result there were many relics such as this hand capstan. Many were rescued for preservation.

The four pitch boilers at Canning Graving Docks were used to boil pitch for covering the hulls of wooden sailing ships under repair. They were cast in 1810.

This is the derelict No.2 Canning Graving Dock. This and the Pilotage Building in the background formed the first phase of the Merseyside Maritime Museum. The sludge in the foreground is concrete waste from a ready-mixed concrete plant on the quay.

This is the same graving dock in 1984 with a fleet of historic boats. Sir Alec Rose's yacht *Lively Lady* is leading. The No.1 dock housed the retired Liverpool pilot vessel *Edmund Gardner*.

On special days it is possible to recreate the hustle and bustle of bygone days, with working cranes, a steam lorry and horse-drawn vehicles.

Inside the Albert Dock building of the Maritime Museum it was possible to create the atmosphere of the dock road at the time of mass emigration to the United States from Liverpool in 1854.

From time to time it is also possible to bring full-sized sailing ships into the dock . Here, the Danish training ship *George Stage* is a beautiful echo of the days of working sailing ships in Liverpool Docks.